WHERE IS GOD?

SARAH MARGARET

INDIA • SINGAPORE • MALAYSIA

Copyright © Sarah Margaret 2023
All Rights Reserved.

ISBN 979-8-88959-641-7

This book has been published with all efforts taken to make the material error-free after the consent of the author. However, the author and the publisher do not assume and hereby disclaim any liability to any party for any loss, damage, or disruption caused by errors or omissions, whether such errors or omissions result from negligence, accident, or any other cause.

While every effort has been made to avoid any mistake or omission, this publication is being sold on the condition and understanding that neither the author nor the publishers or printers would be liable in any manner to any person by reason of any mistake or omission in this publication or for any action taken or omitted to be taken or advice rendered or accepted on the basis of this work. For any defect in printing or binding the publishers will be liable only to replace the defective copy by another copy of this work then available.

Contents

Contents

Introduction

For some very religious people, this may be a very offensive question. They believe God to be a very strict person who is waiting in wrath to punish those who disregard Him. The scriptures also depict such a picture of God. But actually, He is the downright opposite character, filled with joy and laughter, excited about everything at every moment. He is beyond time and space. Nothing can hold Him. He is omnipresent and omniscient. He is present everywhere, and He fills everything. He is the fullness of everything. We need not go searching for Him. We will never find Him until we acknowledge His presence right where we are—within us as our very life and the breath we take every moment and, all around us.

We practise so many religions, each with its own set of rules and regulations to follow and rituals to perform. Yet we are still unhappy and dejected in life. It seems that everything is hopeless. We are not excited about everything. We need something to make us happy. We are not happy as we are. We are always seeking something for our fulfilment. The reason for this is we are not in relationship with God our creator. Like the roots of the trees in the soil, we need to trust God and be rooted in Him for our life. He is our soil. Without Him, we cannot do anything. We need Him every single moment. So we seek Him. We are seeking Him in all the religious places. But we do not find Him. Why? This is the million-dollar question. We shall see the answer for this question in this book. He is so near to us. We shall see how we can realise His presence in us. And how we can live and enjoy each moment of our lives in His loving presence.

What Is Religion?

Since my very young days, I have thought that I am a Christian and that I belong to Jesus, while other people who follow other religions belong to their gods. Then, when I grew up, I had so many questions. How can there be so many gods? How can a loving God take some people to heaven and throw the rest of them into hell? Why are there so many differences in every religion? Why do people hate each other in the name of religion? Why is there so much injustice in this world, and God is not doing anything about it? and many more. I thought that I was the only one to have such questions, and the rest of the world is so happy with their religion that they do not have any questions at all. I was very afraid because of my questions. I could not ask these of anyone as we were told to believe everything taught to us in the church.

I thought that I should read the Bible more and pray more to get answers to my questions or to have faith without any questions. But the more I read the Bible and the more I prayed, the more there were questions. I was overwhelmed by them. I could not stand them anymore. Then I asked God to give me a revelation about who He is. He surprised me by not getting angry at me. And He began to reveal things to me about Himself, making me realise that He was right inside me, loving me unconditionally and with boundless compassion. He is the most loving person I have ever met. I have no words to express His incredible love for me. Not only for me, but for everyone on the planet. He did not get offended by my questions. But He began to reveal Himself to me in various ways, which I shall explain in detail. Actually, He led me step by step and brought me to the place where I am right now. I should say that more than a physical journey, it was a journey in my mind, which we can also say, in my spirit. I realised that I am a beloved child of God. Every single person on this planet, irrespective of who they are and what they have done, is a beloved child of God. His love is unconditional.

First, He took me to different places to show me the various kinds of people and the various kinds of life. I was not aware of so many differences in which people live. Though I have read about this in my textbooks, I was overwhelmed to see all those things I read right before my eyes. India is an amazing country with so many cultures that are very colourful. It was very interesting to meet so many people in just two years. When I got married, my husband was working in the Air Force. I travelled with him to Barmer, Baroda, Chandigarh, and Bangalore. When we were at each of these places, we were able to meet people from many parts of our country living at the Air Force quarters. After meeting more people, my questions about God, religion, the purpose of life on this planet, and so on, increased.

On my religious side, before and after I came back to Chennai, the beloved city where I was born and brought up, He took me to various churches. The more I saw the differences among Christians, the more I had questions. All the injustices I saw around the world were also seen in the churches and in the congregation. Then one by one, He began to answer my questions. The first revelation was about the principle of sowing and reaping, according to which everything has been created. So I realised that whatever we give away through our thoughts, words, and actions will come back to us. You may wonder if it is so, even with our thoughts. Absolutely, our thoughts are very powerful. It can create things that we may not have ever seen or heard.

After this revelation, I spent some time realising how, in my life, I created everything with my thoughts, words, and actions. For example, because my mother was employed in a government office, I desired to do the same. And along with that desire, I wished that I would get an appointment before I could complete my graduation. Everything happened exactly how I desired and wished for. I got appointed to a government office in my final year of under graduation. I joined my department, took leave for the pending education, and completed my degree. Every positive thought and statement I made in my life came true exactly as they were. It was also the same with every negative thing. Whatever news I heard and read in newspapers and other media became my reality as I believed and discussed it. But after I realised the power of my thoughts, words, and actions, I began to stop believing and talking about all the negative things. This was very difficult in the beginning. Even in my actions, I had to be positive, even if my circumstances were negative. But God enabled me to have immense faith in Him through all the spiritual food that I was getting from hearing messages from various people of God.

The second revelation was how much God loves us and how little all religions mention it. Most of the religions and the scriptures reveal Him to be very angry with everyone who disregards Him. But Jesus revealed Him to be the most loving person, whose love for us and everything else he created cannot be compared or described in words. His love is the same even for those who reject Him. Jesus once told a parable about God's love for us. Once, there was a wealthy father with two sons.

The younger son came to him and asked for his portion of the inheritance. The father immediately gave it to him. Soon, the younger son took all his inheritance and went to a faraway country. He lived there wildly and spent all his money. He had nothing left and was also very hungry. So he went looking for a job. He was asked to take care of some pigs. He could not get enough food and desired the food of the pigs. Then he thought about his father, who fed all his servants very well. He came to his senses and decided to go back to his father, thinking that he would ask his father to allow him to be accepted as his servant, at least. But when the father saw his younger son return, he ran to him and hugged and kissed him. He asked the servants to bring a ring for his finger, a coat to wear, and sandals for his feet. He then ordered the servants to kill a calf and make a big feast to celebrate the return of his younger son.

Look how Jesus describes the father's heart being filled with unconditional love and unlimited compassion for his son, irrespective of what he did. I realised that this is the heart of our Heavenly Father. When I realised this, I was filled with great joy and happiness. After listening to all kinds of "not good enough" statements in life, I realised that God has created me to be more than enough in every aspect of my life. It was an absolute "aha" moment for me. And I realised that it is not just for me but for every single person on this planet, irrespective of who they are or what they have done. I began to value every single person, irrespective of who they are or what they have done. This realisation transformed me completely and filled me with awe and wonder about God and about everything in life. Life became exciting for me. Every day is a new day of excitement. I was filled with the unconditional love and unlimited compassion of God for everyone and everything in life.

The third realisation was about what religions and scriptures are all about. Once, I attended a conference on interfaith dialogue. I met people from Buddhism, Christianity, Hinduism, and Islam. They spoke about God, who is above all the religions and has allowed various religions for humanity to seek Him. I realised that all the scriptures are the realisations of different people about God. Irrespective of who they are, they become transformed when they have a personal realisation about God and try to explain it in words. But there are no words to explain the love of God for His creations. He is so excited about everyone and everything. He is just waiting for us to realise His love for us and transform us to be like Him. People have created religions from the experiences of the transformed people recorded in the scriptures. Without a personal realisation of God's love for us, we cannot know Him through any religion.

Where Is Heaven?

We hear so many people going to heaven for a few moments and coming back. A neurological doctor says that he died, went to heaven, and then came back. When he describes heaven, he says that, though he was not a spiritual person and had not sought God all his life, from the moment he entered it, he was filled with love and was filled with the feeling of being loved. No one talked there. They were able to feel and communicate without words. When he came back, he began to tell everyone that they were loved and accepted by God, irrespective of who they were and what they had done. Heaven is a place filled with unconditional love and unlimited compassion in the nature of God, where we will not have a body like we have now. That is after we die here. But the amazing fact is that we can enjoy that heavenly life right now, when we are here in our physical bodies upon this planet.

Jesus said that heaven is right here, inside you. What did He mean by that? He always taught about God, who dwells inside us, irrespective of who we are or what we have done. He is filled with unconditional love and unlimited compassion for everyone and everything He created. Once, Jesus was travelling with His disciples and came to a Samaritan village. In those days, the Jews treated the Samaritans as people unworthy of God. So there was hatred between the two groups. When the disciples went to buy some food, Jesus sat near a well outside the village. A Samaritan woman came to get some water. When she reached the well, Jesus looked at her and asked her for water to drink. She was very surprised, as Jews would never even talk with the Samaritans, and here was Jesus asking for water. So she inquired as to the reason for his request for water from a Samaritan woman. Jesus responded that if she drinks the water He provides, she will never thirst again. She was more surprised and asked Him how He would get water without a rope and a vessel. And Jesus said that if she believed in Him, rivers of living water would flow from her.

When she heard this, she got excited, and she asked for the living water. Jesus asked her to bring her husband. But she said that she did not have a husband. Jesus replied saying that it was true, as she was married to five men and, the one with whom she was now, was not her husband. She was astounded as He revealed everything about her. She ran into the village and told everyone about Him. They all came and heard everything Jesus said. They were very glad and asked Him to stay in their village for a few more days and teach them. Jesus stayed there for a few more days and taught them about the love of God.

Here we see that, though anyone would condemn the Samaritan woman as unworthy of God, not because she was a Samaritan but because she was married to five men and now lives with a person who is not her husband, it was not a problem for Jesus. He did not condemn her, but instead offered her the living water. By living water, He meant the Spirit of God that is in every single person. But we are not able to recognise Him when we think that God is somewhere outside and is very angry with everyone who has disregarded Him. If we could believe that the Spirit of God is in us with unconditional love and unlimited compassion, we would be able to enjoy His loving presence, and we would be excited about everything in life because He would be overflowing through us.

The Samaritan woman could not realise the spirit of God dwelling in her because she trusted in all the physical things she saw before her. Though she had problems with everything she trusted, she did not stop to think about it until Jesus stopped her. Then she realised she had made the mistake of trusting in everything other than God. When she realised it, she surrendered her life to God and became very happy and excited. She began to tell everyone about this realisation of God living inside her and experiencing her life with her.

We were all connected to Him at our birth. But we gradually became disconnected, believing that He was somewhere outside. He is continuously speaking with us in our conscience. Unfortunately, we reject His voice in our ignorance, His love for us, and His presence within us. The more we reject, the more we become exhausted in life, without knowing why. Furthermore, we begin to observe the world around us from the moment we arrive on this planet. We see that people live only with what they can observe with their five senses.

We do not see that we have been created to be powerful in our thoughts, words, and deeds. As a result, they can create anything. We begin to believe only in the physical things we see. We are not able to believe in far greater things that cannot be seen but can be created if we think we can. Only if we listen to His loving voice in our conscience will we be able to make the right choices every moment, trusting in Him.

God is not angry about our wrong choices. He knows that we make the wrong choices because of our ignorance of His love for us. He is not worried about our wrong choices. Freedom of choice is His design for our lives. He is filled with unconditional love and unlimited compassion for all of us. He is waiting for us to realise His presence within us and everywhere around us. When we realise His presence within us and all around us, we will be filled with immense joy and happiness at every moment of our lives. We will not have anything to worry about in life, as He will take care of everything. He is more powerful than the most powerful thing that we may fear in life. We will be filled with unconditional love and unlimited compassion for everyone and everything around us. We will not be able to hurt or harm anyone. And nothing around us will be able to hurt or harm us. Life will be very exciting, with nothing to fear or worry about. Isn't this amazing? This is the amazing and wonderful heavenly life that we have been designed to live.

But why do we not experience this? No religion has the answer for this, as they mostly talk about God being somewhere else. Unless we believe in His presence within us and all around us, we will not be able to be free from all kinds of fears, worries, and anxieties. That is why Jesus said to the Jews that the kingdom of God is within them. They thought that God was somewhere in the heavens, in the mountains, or in the temple, without realising His presence within them and all around them. Every scripture is filled with the experiences of people who believed in this loving presence of God and did great things in life. Right from the ordinary people to the kings, everyone experienced His loving presence and did mighty things with great love for others. We will be able to do more only if we believe in His presence. That is why Jesus said that if we believe in Him, we will do greater things. So, where is heaven? It is right there within you when you believe in His loving presence. Wherever you are, that place will be transformed into the likeness of heaven, filled with unconditional love and unlimited compassion.

Without fear of anyone or anything on this planet, life would be very exciting. We will be filled with unconditional love. Whatever we do, we will do in love. Even in our thoughts, we will be filled with unconditional love. Our circumstances will provide us with the same. We will not be able to hurt anyone with our thoughts, words, and deeds. We will be able to realise that whatever people do against us is because of their ignorance of this amazing life we have been created to live and enjoy. So heaven is right where we are. It is an experience, not a place. Right now, if you are living like this, then you are living a heavenly life. Some experience heaven right here on this planet, while others experience it after their physical death.

Where Is Hell?

After reading the previous chapter, we would have completely forgotten about "hell." If God is present within us and everywhere around us, "Where is hell?" will be our question. But most religions talk about hell. You will be completely shocked to hear that hell is also within us and all around us. If we do not believe in God's presence within us and all around us, we will experience hell right here. No one would be able to accept this, as we all think that hell is a place somewhere. a dark and fiery place. Don't we? But that is not true. If we do not believe that God is within us and all around us, we will experience hell in our minds at all times and in all circumstances. So the basic factor in experiencing either heaven or hell is the realisation of God's presence in our lives. Isn't this unbelievable? But this is the truth. Let us see how.

We have been created to live with freedom of choice. As we saw earlier, we are connected to God at our birth. But when we take in everything around us with our five senses, we begin to believe in those things more than we believe in listening to the loving voice of God in our conscience. Thereby, we begin to do as per the voice of this world, which seems very appropriate. Unfortunately, in our ignorance about the love of God, we first reject Him in our conscience. Thus, we lose our peace in Him and begin to experience fear, worry, and anxiety about everything in life. Then we do everything as per what we observe from the world outside and make the wrong choices in ignorance. Finally, as per the principle of the law of attraction, what we give will come back to us, making our lives hell. Despite our best efforts to appear healthy, we gradually lose energy and become ill, first in our minds and then in our bodies. We first experience hell in our minds, then in our bodies. It is all about our choices. If we choose to reject Him in our conscience, we will experience hell.

For example, we have been created to trust in God for everything—every single moment in life. But we trust in every living and non-living thing in life more than in God. Then we begin to live with expectations about them. We are sure to get disappointed, as our lives have been designed to be lived with trust in God. Because of the freedom of choice, people tend to change, and so God did not design us to trust anything around us. God will never change. So we can trust in Him completely. But everything else can change depending on the circumstances. Then our disappointment will become depression and dejection in life. We will become sick in our minds, and later we will also be affected in our bodies. Whereas, when we trust in God for our lives, everything will work out very well for us without any problems. If you trust in God more than all other things, you will be experiencing heaven right now.

But many of us don't experience heaven right now. Is there any hope for us? That is the million-dollar question. Of course, by the grace of God, we have hope for complete restoration so we can experience heaven right here on this planet. As we have seen earlier, He is not angry about our wrong choices. Making the wrong choices doesn't only mean committing serious crimes such as stealing and murder. It is also very simple, like being disrespectful and lying to people around us who completely believe in us. But God knows that we do such things in ignorance of His love for us. So He is patiently waiting for us to return to Him, to restore us to being like Him, full of unconditional love and boundless compassion for everyone and everything around us. We will be able to make the right choices every moment of our life, listening to His loving voice in our conscience. Life will be amazing and wonderful, free from all fears, worries, and anxieties. We will be free from all kinds of limitations, restrictions, and expectations and have complete freedom in everything to be who we are in His love.

As long as we make the right choices, we will be free from all kinds of sickness and disease in this world. These are hellish experiences. Health and well-being are heavenly experiences. We experience hell because of our ignorance about the heavenly life right here. Every single person is enabled to realise this at some point in their life. The more we reject Him, the greater our struggle will be. As we are not aware of this, we actually reject Him in ignorance. So the good news of God's love for humanity should be proclaimed to humanity. We are beating and nailing Him to the cross by rejecting His voice in our conscience. Actually, we are the losers. We lose our lives and live like zombies here. But when we realise our rejection of God in our conscience, we will be restored completely to our original life at birth. We will be filled with the overflowing life of God and with complete joy and happiness. We will be excited about everything in life.

Our family life will be very exciting. Our work will be very exciting. Our social life will be very exciting. Everything will make us happy, and everything will fill us with hope. We will be able to create everything we desire with our thoughts, words, and deeds. Nothing will be impossible for us. Life will be amazing. This is the desire of God for us. Though He designed us to be like this, we lose it in our ignorance. But we are provided with chances to turn back to Him and be restored to our original lives. We will be a blessing to ourselves and to the world around us. What do you want? Heaven or hell? Hell is also not a place but an experience. It is in your mind. Just believe in God, who is in you, filled with unconditional love and unlimited compassion for you. You will experience heaven right here.

Where Is The Devil?

The Devil is nowhere. But you can create him in your mind. Everything that binds you is a devil. Whatever you believe in, other than God, your creator is a devil. When you believe in God, you will create heaven right here. But if you believe in other things or other people, then those things and those people will become the devil, and you will create hell right here. Isn't this unbelievable? But it is a fact. Most religions talk about him as a person, but he is just an imaginary person and not a real person. Those who do not believe in God will live in fear of everything, making their lives a living hell and creating various types of devils. I grew up in a Christian family and have heard so much preaching about the devil and his atrocities. I also believed them and suffered so much in my mind. In the Bible, the devil is wonderfully explained as a person who tries to grab the place of God and is knocked down to be no more when we trust in God for our lives. As long as we keep something else in the place of God, we will suffer. If we keep God in the right place, we will be able to enjoy life. Without knowing this, I created so many devils in my mind. But now, after realising that there is no devil, I am totally free and happy.

It is very important that we understand that the devil is not there and that he is only created in our minds as long as we believe in everything else except God. I am very glad that God enabled me to realise this so that I can explain it to my fellow beings. We have been created to enjoy life every moment, trusting and experiencing God, and not to live in fear every moment, trusting other things. You might be wondering what kinds of devils are created in our minds. It depends on what each person puts their trust in. It could be a person, or a job, or a qualification, or a piece of property, or money, or a caste, or a community, or a nation, and the list goes on and on. It can also be any religion in which other aspects of that religion take the place of God. These are the different kinds of raw materials needed to create the devil.

Even I created so many devils and suffered because of them until I trusted God. The moment I put my trust in God, all the devils just vanished. It is very simple. Anyone can get rid of all the devils in their life. When we put our trust in God, all the people and things that have made our lives a living hell will begin to transform themselves into heaven. This is very amazing. This is very real. God is so good and so loving that He has given us complete authority over our lives. We can create anything we want. God is not angry with us, even though we have created so many devils and made our lives a living hell. He is just waiting for us to realise our ignorance and turn back to Him. He is waiting with unconditional love and unlimited compassion to restore us to be like Him, in His nature, in which we were created in our mother's womb.

Your life is in your hands. Do not give your authority to anything or any person around you. Use your authority to create an amazing life by trusting God. You will not have anything to fear. You will be free from all kinds of fears, anxieties, and worries. You will be free from all kinds of limitations, expectations, and restrictions. Life would be very exciting at every moment. You will be a blessing to yourself and the world around you. Everything and everyone around you will be a blessing to you.

What Is The Purpose Of Life?

Once I went to an interfaith dialogue conference in which people from Hinduism, Buddhism, Christianity, and Islam attended. A speaker from the Islamic faith said that the purpose of human life is to serve each other. I was stunned for a second. Is it so simple? I thought that the purpose of life was very huge and complicated. It varies from person to person, place to place, religion to religion, and country to country. But it is very simple. We are here to serve each other. God has created everything to be very simple and easy. But in our ignorance, we have complicated everything and made life very tough.

How do we serve each other? At any point in history, we see that people either lived in small groups or large communities. Even though we are a small family, we rely on so many people for even the most basic of needs. For example, if we want to have a cup of coffee, we need so many people to work for us to get us the milk, sugar, coffee powder, and the cup in which we drink it. Without them, even if we have money, we cannot drink a cup of coffee. It is the same for everything in life. We need so many people for everything we do in life. So whatever they do in life is serving people in some way. In the same way, we have to serve one another so that we can live a social life without any problems. If it is so, whatever everyone is doing in their occupation is serving others. Serving one another is the purpose of life on this planet.

God has an amazing plan and purpose for our lives on this planet. It is to be like Him. We can divide it into four categories.

- The first is to be like Him, filled with unconditional love and unlimited compassion for everyone and everything around us, so that we can live free from all kinds of fear, worry, and anxiety.

- The second is to be happy and enjoy life every moment, listening to His loving voice in our conscience, so that we will make the right choices every moment, which results in happiness and joy every moment, irrespective of our circumstances.

- The third one is to have freedom of choice in everything we do. So that we can live free from all kinds of limitations, restrictions, and expectations.

- The fourth is to create everything we desire in life with our thoughts, words, and actions. As a result, everything we do and have in our lives will be exciting.

Let us now examine each of the categories of life's purpose in greater depth.

1. We have been created to be like our creator in every aspect of our lives. Unconditional love and unlimited compassion can be declared as the origin of our life. Because this is what God is. He accepts everything as it is. He has no expectations. He has no restrictions. And He has no limitations. He has only love for everyone and everything He created. He has created us with His love in our mother's womb. We lived in this love as babies for a short time. But when we grow up taking in everything around us through our five senses, we lose this love because of our fear, worry, and anxiety about everything. Depending upon the circumstances in which we grow, we differ in our behaviour and attitude as we are moulded by our circumstances. Some may think deeply at an early age and come to the realisation of God's love for us, irrespective of who we are or what we have done. Some may take time to realise this. The realisation of God's love for us will restore us to our original state of

unconditional love and unlimited compassion for everyone and everything around us. We will be filled with love and be able to accept everyone, irrespective of who they are or what they have done. This is the purpose of our life, which will enable us to be free from all kinds of fears, worries, and anxieties.

2. Happiness is all we desire in life. It is the purpose of God for our lives. Isn't it unbelievable? Most religions show an angry or unhappy God. But actually, He desires our happiness and wants us to enjoy every moment of our lives. He is so excited and happy about our lives, irrespective of who we are or what we have done in life. As I have said in a previous chapter about a parable of Jesus where the father is never angry with what his son did, He was only waiting for his son to realise his mistake. God is not about asking us why we made some mistake, but he desires that we realise our mistake by asking ourselves why we made that mistake. As we see in the parable, our Heavenly Father is waiting for us to turn back to Him, and be restored to being like Him. Listening to His voice in our conscience, we will be able to make the right choices, and enjoy every moment of life with great excitement and happiness about everything in life. We will be happy regardless of our circumstances because we will trust in our Creator more than everything else around us.

3. The third purpose of our lives is to have the ability to choose what we do in life. We have been created to have freedom of choice in everything we do every moment of our lives, irrespective of what our choice is. In the beginning, as a little baby, we made the right choices, hearing the loving voice of God in our conscience, until we were disturbed by the voice of this world. We started to observe everything around us through our five senses and were greatly confused. The voice of God inside us tells us to make the right choices. But the world around us has given us some wrong ideas about life, and because of its pressure, we choose them even if they are wrong. For example, though we know it is not right to see differences among the people based on religion, community, caste, race, and so on, we make the wrong choice of treating people differently based on the above facts. It is because of the circumstances in which we grew up. We believe that treating people differently is not wrong, as we have seen from the beginning. Because of this, we have made the wrong choices, rejecting the loving voice of God in our conscience to treat people equally. We have become hopeless and confused, and we are in fear every moment. We are not able to accept anyone or believe in anyone.

But a little baby does not reject anyone. He or she is unaware of any variations in anything. We may be wondering how we made the wrong choices. As I previously stated, it could be due to what we observe from day one and believe to be correct when, in fact, it is incorrect, like treating people with differences. This may be because of our culture, our society, our nationality, and so on. In our ignorance, we may have made poor decisions. Until we become like God we make wrong choices in ignorance. Just trusting in God's love for us will transform us to be like Him filled with unconditional love and unlimited compassion for everyone and everything around us.

Fortunately, we have been created to have freedom of choice and can choose what we want at every moment. What we choose becomes our life. The amazing part is, as we have seen in the parable of Jesus about the rich father, that God is waiting for us to realise our wrong choices and turn back to Him. He desires to restore us to being like Him, filled with unconditional love and unlimited compassion for everyone and everything around us. His love for us forgives all our wrong choices and treats us as if we have not made any wrong choices at all. This may not be acceptable in our systems, where there is punishment for every wrong choice, regardless of whether the person realises their mistake. But the heavenly system is entirely different, which can be understood only when we realise God's love for us and for everyone. We will be able to accept and believe everyone without any problem. We will be free from all kinds of fears. We will become unlimited and overflowing in the nature of our creator. We will become free from all kinds of restrictions and expectations. This is the desire of God for us.

4. The fourth purpose of life is to create everything we desire with our thoughts, words, and deeds. We may wonder how it is possible. It is God's design for our lives. Whatever we think, say, and do will come back to us as our life. Isn't this amazing? Fortunately, this is a fact. If we sit back and remember everything that has happened in our lives, we will be able to realise that all that we desired would have been fulfilled if we had thought, spoken, and done everything positive about them. But if we had negative thoughts, words, or actions about them, we would have suffered much because of it. For example, Shri Abdul Kalam desired to fly when he was in school in a small town, and he eventually became a scientist irrespective of his circumstances. He became the President of India and made a great impact on millions of young people. In the same way, if we have a difficulty in our life and consider it a problem, we would be completely dejected and depressed by it. But if we consider it a challenge and an opportunity to go to the next level in life, we would have overcome it very easily. So, we have been created to enjoy life every moment with great joy and excitement, creating everything we desire.

The most important point about this aspect is that whatever we desire should be a blessing to us and to the world around us. If our desire is not beneficial to either, then we will suffer because of it, and so will the world around us. Hence, it is very important that our desire should be a blessing and not a suffering. Our life is what we think, speak, and do. Even if, because of our circumstances, we have made some wrong choices in ignorance but realise it and turn back to God, He will bless us and make us a blessing to the world around us. He will reveal Himself through us and enjoy our life with us as He dwells in us with love as our very life.

Who Are You?

From day one, we are being told by everyone around us about who we should be. When we listen to all of them, we actually get diverted from who we are and try to be like someone else. Success in life comes from being who we are completely. So first let us see who we are, and then we shall see how we get diverted from it and how we can get back to it. Who we are is nothing but our desires that come from within our hearts in response to our lives. Life is given by God to us when we were formed in our mother's womb. He dwells in us as our very life and is also all around us. He enables us to live and do everything we desire within our circumstances.

We have been created with freedom of choice. We can choose whatever we want at every moment. Whether it is a good choice or a bad choice, we are free to make any choice we want. It may seem very unfair, as people may make the wrong choices and bring suffering. Even if we call something suffering, it may also be called a challenge to be overcome. If we call it a challenge, we will be able to overcome it and go to the next level in life. If we call it a problem or suffering, we will not progress in life. At the same time, those who make the wrong choices will have to receive them back, as we have been created on the principle of sowing and reaping. Whatever we give, whether good or bad, will come back to us. When we make the right decisions, regardless of our circumstances, we will reap the benefits many times over.

As we are not aware of this, we make the wrong choices in ignorance and suffer because of that. Moreover, if we do not listen to the loving voice of God in our conscience and give in to the pressure from around us, we will definitely be making the wrong choices. But God is not angry about our choices, as He has created us with freedom of choice. He is just waiting for us to come back to Him after realising our wrong choices, like the younger son in the parable told by Jesus. If we turn back to Him, we will be restored to our original pattern of being like Him, filled with unconditional love and unlimited compassion towards everyone and everything in life. This is how we were created to live.

The second important thing about who we are is that we need to do what we desire from our hearts and not what other people say. Our desires are always good. But the choices we make to fulfil our desires make the difference in whether they are good or bad. For example, we desire to buy something, and we work for it. After getting the required money, we will go and buy it. Then it is a good desire. At the same time, if we do not want to work and try to get it by other means, like stealing or by demanding and commanding, then it becomes a bad desire. Hence, the difference is in the choices we make to fulfil our desire. When we desire a job. It is a good desire, as long as we do our job well. If we neglect our jobs, it will become a bad desire. When we choose to make anything out of good desire, we will be happy and successful, irrespective of our circumstances. However, if we choose to make anything out of bad desire through our wrong choices, we will be unhappy and depressed, even if our circumstances are favourable.

Sometimes we desire to do something. But the people around us reject our desire and pressurise us to do something else that we may not like. If we choose to do what others want us to do, we will be unhappy and dejected in life. So we need to be very careful to do what we want to do in life and never try to do what others do or be like others. Every choice we make should be based on our own desires. We should also be careful to listen to the loving voice of God in our conscience every moment and make the right choices. Then we will be very happy and satisfied with life. There won't be any need to ask God for anything. He will provide us with more than everything we may need. He will make the universe work for us.

Hence, the answer to the question "Who are we?" is everything we want, choose, think, say, and do. For example, look at our body. As babies, we were quite small. We grew day by day, thanks to the food we ate every day. So we got our bodies from what we ate. Similarly, everything we do at every moment creates us. The more we listen to our conscience, the greater will be our happiness. The more we reject our conscience, the greater our unhappiness will be. Most religions say that our lives are decided by God and we have nothing to do with them; we just fulfil His desire. But actually, God has given us the ability to decide everything in our lives. He has granted freedom of choice through the sowing and reaping principle. There is complete freedom and happiness in the plan of God for us. He just desires to experience life through us. He is willing to experience anything we choose. We can choose to make Him happy by making the right choices in our lives, or we can choose to make Him sad and suffer by making the wrong ones. He is not angry with our choices. But He is just accepting us as we are. He is waiting with unconditional love and unlimited compassion for us to realise our wrong choices and turn back to Him. Turning back to Him is the key to an abundant life with unlimited happiness.

Why Pain?

I was really surprised when I heard for the first time that pain has a purpose. You may wonder what the purpose of pain is. For example, when we accidentally touch a hot vessel, we feel the pain and immediately remove our hand. If there is no pain, we will not be able to realise that we are touching a hot vessel, and without moving away from it, our hand would be damaged more. So, pain exists to teach us something in life. Whether it is a pain in our body or a pain in our spirit, it has a purpose. From day one, we experience so many varieties of pain, both physically and mentally. First, let us see how our physical pain helps us.

When we have a headache, it is not because that part of our body is not well and is in pain. As the centre of our nervous system, there are numerous causes of pain in our heads. So, if there is a problem in any part of our body, it will be reflected in our head. Hence, we need to check for the problem in our entire body rather than taking pills for headaches, which are very harmful. Thus, by taking pills for a headache, we are creating a new problem while the actual problem exists somewhere else without being treated. You may wonder how we can be free from this kind of physical pain. We shall deal with it in a separate chapter on sickness.

In the same way, when we have pain in our mind because of some incident, we need to understand that the pain is caused by some other problem in us that needs to be treated. You may wonder what other problems can cause us pain when something happens to us. First, we need to realise the purpose of our lives and live them as per that purpose. We have seen in an earlier chapter how we are here to serve each other. We can do this by realising God's purpose for our lives: to be like Him in nature, filled with unconditional love and unlimited compassion for everyone and everything around us. We will be able to enjoy life while trusting Him and creating everything as per our desire with our thoughts and our actions. We will be free from all kinds of limitations, restrictions, and expectations as we are created to have freedom of choice every moment.

So, if we are not living our lives as per this loving design of God for our lives, we will be in pain whenever something happens against us. When we use our freedom of choice properly, no one will be able to hurt or harm us. Even if they are doing something against us using their freedom of choice, it is actually against themselves, as it is going to come back to them in many folds. We will be protected by God in amazing ways beyond our thoughts and imaginations. Hence, we need not be in pain over what others are doing, as they are going to get it back. We have to realise that we can enjoy every moment of life by trusting God. Nothing has the power to hurt or harm us, as we will be above our circumstances with higher thoughts and desires if we use our freedom of choice properly.

How can we use our freedom of choice properly? Just by making the right choices, which will be a blessing to us and to everyone around us, We must be mindful of our choices at all times. Though our circumstances may be very tough and hopeless, we need to trust in God, who is right within us and all around us with unconditional love and unlimited compassion for us. We need to take care to listen to His loving voice in our conscience and make the right choices, trusting Him, even if the whole world is making wrong choices. Then we will experience Him in our lives, working for us in impossible ways. We see this in all the scriptures as experienced by various people who trusted God even in hopeless circumstances.

So pain is not something that happens to us. It is due to our ignorance of all the amazing and wonderful designs of life given to us by our Creator as a result of His incredible love for us. If we just realise all these things as per the design of God for us, we will be able to be free from pain. We will trust God every moment and make the right choices, listening to His loving voice in our conscience. We will not be able to hurt anyone. No one will be able to harm us because God protects us when we completely trust Him. We will be a blessing to us and to the world around us. Pain is not bad or evil. It is actually good to make us realise that something is wrong. If we give ourselves some time to think about it, it helps us realise what is wrong and become free from pain in life.

Why Suffering?

Once, a king wanted to know how responsible his people were in their everyday lives. So one night, he took a big stone and put it in the middle of a road. He also kept a pot of gold coins with a small note in it under the stone. It was written in the note that the pot of gold belongs to the person who moves the stone. So the next day he was watching, and the people were walking around the stone. No one was willing to lift the stone. So in the evening, the King called the people together and asked for the stone to be removed. As the stone was moved, everyone was amazed to see a pot beneath it. When they realised that the pot of gold coins was for the person who may have removed the stone, they felt bad that they were lazy and irresponsible, and because of that, they missed the opportunity to receive a pot of gold coins.

Similarly, in life, we receive many opportunities for blessing. But we do not use those opportunities and keep blaming everyone instead of using the blessings given to us. It may be in our family life, or in our work life, or in our social life. Are we trying to walk around the stone or are we trying to remove the stone? This is very important. When we try to walk around the stone, we reject the blessing beneath the stone. The unmoved stone stays in our lives as a source of suffering. All our lives, we will be walking around such stones, blaming everyone around us for that. If we do not learn our lesson, the lesson will repeat itself for as long as we do not learn it.

The second reason for our suffering is not doing what we have to do because of our laziness, a negative attitude toward others, or being self-centered. For example, if we are to sanction a loan to someone and we delay it because of any of the above-mentioned reasons, the beneficiary will be delayed in whatever he has planned to do with it. If he or she trusts God for his or her life, then God will make a way for them and enable them to do everything as per their plan. We may have other reasons for our delay in sanctioning the loan, like ego and arrogance. Ego arises from our attitude toward that person. Arrogance is the result of overestimating oneself. How can this cause us to suffer? This world has been created on the principle of sowing and reaping. As we have sown delay with this, we will reap delay in everything in life. Our suffering will not end until we realise our wrong choices and turn back to God.

The third cause of our suffering is our belief that suffering is more important than faith in God. Because of that, when we listen to the media, we keep believing that we will also suffer like other people who suffer because of their ignorance about trusting God more than everything in this world. Trusting in God is the key to our lives. If we trust in God and make the right choices, listening to His loving voice in our conscience, we will be able to enjoy life, free from all kinds of suffering. But if we believe in suffering more than we trust in God, we will be suffering all the time until we realise our distrust in God and turn back to Him.

We suffer in life in ignorance because we are unaware of all the causes of our suffering. Though we desire a life free from suffering, we are not able to live one. First, we need to use all our opportunities for blessing. Second, we need to do our duties without delay. Third, we need to trust in God more than the suffering we see around us. God is not angry about our wrong choices. He desires to deliver us from all our sufferings. The only key to this is to turn back to Him after realising all our wrong choices. He will transform us, to be like Him and make the right choices at all times. We will be able to live a life free from all kinds of suffering. Hence, suffering is nothing but ignorance about God's love for us.

Why Sickness?

There are many reasons for sickness. We shall see about a few of them in this chapter. The primary reason for sickness is our diet. Eating too much or too little is dangerous and will harm our health. In the same way, if we are not taking balanced foods with all the minerals and vitamins that we require, we will get sick because of their deficiency. Furthermore, eating when we aren't hungry or not eating when we are hungry is a major contributor to our illness. Even if we eat a balanced diet, we still need to chew our food properly in order to benefit from the vitamins and minerals in it. Basically, if we are careful regarding our diet in all the above-mentioned ways, we will be free from sickness.

The second reason for our sickness is that we are depressed mentally due to various circumstances in life. When we are depressed, our body automatically becomes sick. Why do we get depressed? It may be because of various discriminations in life based on gender, caste, community, nationality, education, occupation, money, power, and so on. All these things will make a person hopeless in life, and he or she will become depressed and dejected in life. Though there are so many things that cause depression in life, if we realise the unconditional love and unlimited compassion of God towards us, irrespective of who we are or what we have done, we will be able to be free from all kinds of dejections and depressions in life. We will be able to enjoy every moment of life while trusting God for everything.

You may wonder how we can trust in the unconditional love and unlimited compassion of God in such a hopeless situation. It may seem to be hopeless for us. But God is able to turn all hopelessness into an abundance of life. For example, a boy whose parents were beggars was interested in studying, even though he lived in the streets without a house. When a priest from an NGO said that he would help him study, he immediately used that opportunity and began to study well. Later, he was accepted to one of Italy's universities and went abroad to study. In this way, if we trust in God, we will be able to overcome any hopeless situation in life. Trust in God is the key to a life free from all kinds of limitations, restrictions, and expectations.

The third reason for our illness is that we believe in all kinds of sickness more than we believe in God. The media keeps talking about all the various kinds of sickness so much that we start to believe that we are affected by sickness more than we trust God for a life free from sickness. How can trust in God enable us to be free from sickness? God is the source of our very life and breath. He is all around us, filled with unconditional love and unlimited compassion for us. He desires that our lives be free from sickness. If we believe in Him, we will be able to live a healthy life free of illness.

The fourth reason is that we do not give our bodies enough rest. Anything gets worn out if we keep using it continuously. It has to be replaced after some time. But our body has been created in such an amazing way that it gets restored to its original state if adequate rest is taken. After providing adequate food for our bodies, we must provide adequate work for our bodies. It should be according to the needs of our body. It should not be less or more than the requirements of our body. And then, if the body is given adequate rest as and when required, it will be in excellent health.

Thus, a sickness-free life is possible if we first follow the proper diet, which includes all of the necessary minerals and vitamins, and eat at the right times. Secondly, to trust in God more than our circumstances, with respect to how people treat us. And thirdly, we have to trust in God more, irrespective of what the media and others say about sickness. Fourthly, we need to take adequate rest. We will be free from all kinds of sickness. Even if we are ignorant about all these things and have fallen sick because of them, if we just realise our ignorance and turn back to God, He will deliver us from all our sickness and restore us completely to be like a little child filled with excellent health.

God Is Everywhere

He is our life, and we live and move through Him. Without Him, we cannot do anything with our body. He is within us to sustain us and all around us to create everything for us. Though He continues to speak to us through our conscience, He leaves us to our choices. No conditions. No restrictions. No limitations. No expectations. We can just do whatever we want at every moment. He does not like to ask why we did something. Rather, He likes to wait until we ask ourselves why we did that thing. He is such an amazing person. There are no words to explain His love for us. He is beyond everything we have and know. He desires for us to expand in every aspect and create new things at every moment. He desires for us a life filled with excitement.

We may wonder what He will do when we make the wrong choices. He will experience all our wrong choices. This is what Jesus came to show the world. We believe that some Roman soldiers nailed Jesus to a cross. But He allows Himself to be beaten, disregarded, and finally nailed to a cross by every single person on this planet. We do this by rejecting His loving voice in our conscience. The more we reject Him, the more we hurt Him. He accepts His hurts because of His love for us, and this is shown by His prayer that we need to be forgiven as we do not know what we are doing. The more we hurt Him, the greater will be our unhappiness. We will be losing our lives little by little. We will continue to lose our lives until we realise our wrong choices. Finally when we turn back to Him, He restores us completely to the original life we had when we were created by Him in our mother's womb. This is what Jesus demonstrated through His resurrection.

But what we do is just lose our lives completely and die physically without allowing ourselves to be restored to be like Him. The transformation or resurrection of our body will make us become spiritual in our body. We will be able to move through walls like Jesus did after the resurrection. This is His desire for us. Some people have undergone this transformation and travelled anywhere they wanted without a vehicle. This will happen to those who believe in such a resurrection or transformation of our physical body into a spiritual body. For a resurrected life, we may not need anything we need now for our physical body. We can go into space without needing oxygen. We will also be beyond time and space, like our creator. Though this happens to us after the death of our physical body, His desire is for us to experience this without experiencing death. That is why it is said that Jesus conquered death.

You may ask how long we can live in our resurrected bodies. Jesus is still living with His resurrected body. Likewise, the other people who were resurrected to a spiritual body can stay here on this planet as long as they want. They can leave the planet and go wherever they want. There are people like this in the Bible, and I believe they are there in other scriptures and other belief systems as well. As we do not spend enough time on our spiritual being, we are not aware of this. Even when people who witnessed it speak about it and it is recorded in the scriptures, we associate it with other things and are satisfied with the explanations we receive from religious leaders.

So, what should we do to have a spiritual body? Jesus said that you should become like a little child. He never said that you should pray more, read the Bible more, give more offerings, or fast more to enter the kingdom of God. He did not speak about a kingdom away from this world. He was always talking about the Kingdom life on this planet. He showed how to live the kingdom life by delivering people from all their unhappiness.

Life in the kingdom will be full of joy. It will be filled with unconditional love and unlimited compassion for everyone and everything around us. Some believed in everything He said and experienced the Kingdom life right then. They did so many miracles and travelled far and wide, speaking about this amazing kingdom life. Thomas was one of them, and he came to India and visited some other Asian countries also. He did so many miracles that half the population of India became Christians at that time, as said by Swami Vivekananda in his book "Gnanadeepam."

Kingdom life is not about doing some rituals or having a church membership. Even a non-Christian can live a kingdom life if he recognises his wrong choices and repents. In His Sermon on the Mount, Jesus describes Kingdom life. It is not about doing some rituals and entering the kingdom. But it is about entering the Kingdom, and then our lives automatically become the sermon on the mount. We do not need to learn the Sermon on the Mount to live like that. We just have to believe that God dwells in us and realise our wrong choices because we have rejected Him in our conscience. We will then be restored to being like Him, and our lives will become the Sermon on the Mount. We will be able to make the right choices by listening to Him in our conscience.

God is everywhere, and it is just that, whether we acknowledge Him or not. His loving presence is all over the place. He is overflowing with nature. We can see this in nature. Look at the trees. just one seed. How many fruits and how many trees it produces. Unlimited. It goes on and on. He desires our lives to be like that, overflowing in every aspect of our life. Let us open our hearts to this overflowing life. Let every single person upon this planet realise this and live an overflowing life as per the design of God for us and His amazing love.

Thus, a sickness-free life is possible if we first follow the proper diet, which includes all of the necessary minerals and vitamins, and eat at the right times. Secondly, to trust in God more than our circumstances, with respect to how people treat us. And thirdly, we have to trust in God more, irrespective of what the media and others say about sickness. Fourthly, we need to take adequate rest. We will be free from all kinds of sickness. Even if we are ignorant about all these things and have fallen sick because of them, if we just realise our ignorance and turn back to God, He will deliver us from all our sickness and restore us completely to be like a little child filled with excellent health.

You Create Your World

From day one on this planet we create our own world. We have been created with this amazing and wonderful power to create our own world. It is not the same for everyone. It differs from person to person.It depends upon the way we desire, believe, imagine, and do things. Jesus said that if you tell the mountain to move and fall into the ocean and believe that it will happen, then it will happen as you have said. Such is the power we have been created with. Sometimes we see that people are making very extraordinary claims about doing something. Though it seems impossible at that time, we find it happening in due course. And we are baffled.

We create our world by relying on three major factors. Our thoughts, words, and actions At first, it was very difficult for me to believe this fact. But when I spent some time looking back at my life, I realised that it is very true. It was amazing to realise that our thoughts have so much power and they are able to create everything exactly as we think. Prayer can be said as a declaration of what we desire. The only condition for this is to continuously think, speak, and do everything positive about it. Negative thoughts, words, and actions have the power to destroy any good thing upon this planet. So it is very important that we think, speak, and act positively every moment of our lives.

For example, if we trust in God for our lives and believe that He will take care of everything in them, we will make the right choices every moment, listening to the loving voice of God in our conscience. We will be creating a world free from pain, sickness, hunger, hatred, anger, fear, worry, and anxiety. It will be heaven on earth. But if we do not trust in God and trust in all the things of this world, we will not be able to listen to the loving voice of God in our conscience and will make wrong choices every moment while listening to everything around us. We will be creating a world filled with pain, sickness, hunger, hatred, anger, fear, worry, and anxiety. It will be hell on earth. Trust in God is the key, and it will bring healing, health, joy, happiness, and love into our world.

We can create the devil in this world by trusting everything in it. It could be people, money, family, a job, a community, a nation, a race, a religion, or anything else in which we place our trust. In the wilderness, Jesus, as a human being, realised that the world was trying to take the place of God in the minds of people. It is the only problem for a human being. Everything we put our trust in becomes our devil, who will control us without our permission. This is referred to as being possessed by the devil. Jesus delivered such people and made them realise that trust in God will enable them to enjoy every moment of their life. Apart from these, we also create devils from our fears, worries, and anxieties about various things. By doing so, we make our lives a living hell and blame the devil, who is not present but rather someone we created in our world. Why do we not see the devil in everyone's life universally? Because it is not created by everyone and is only created by a few people who believe in all these kinds of devils. Addiction to anything in this world is as terrible as addiction to alcohol and drugs. Even I created so many devils in my ignorance about the love of God for me, and I lived in fear of everything. For example, if I think someone or something is going to harm me, then that person or thing becomes the devil or a negative energy and will really harm me. Everything happens based on energy, which is created by our thoughts. There is so much power in whatever we do, especially our thoughts. Then, when I realised that there is actually no devil and that it is just the energy I created by my negative thoughts, I put my trust in God, and all the devils just vanished. The basic raw material for creating the devil is fear—fear of losing something or fear of something happening. It may be anything that I mentioned earlier. Trust in God will deliver us from this fear and will fill us with unconditional love and unlimited compassion for everyone and everything around us.

If we believe that everything is good, goodness will be our experience at every moment. If we believe that everything is worse, then we will be experiencing that every moment. It may be in our personal life, in our family life, in our work life, in our social life, in our political life, or in our economic life. Anything in life depends on what we believe, and our world will be created as per our beliefs. It is amazing to realise that our lives are completely within our control. God's love has given us this ability by creating us in His image and likeness, to create everything we desire by our thoughts, words and actions. It is our responsibility to create our world, and no one else can do it for us.

I am greatly amazed by the power of my thoughts, words, and actions to create a world of my own for me. When I think of something, it has the power to change everything in my circumstances to fulfil it, irrespective of the circumstances. I have mentioned earlier about a boy who was born into a family of beggars but went to study in Italy because he desired great things in life. That is the power we have been created with. Nobody talks about this power because we haven't fully realised its potential. It is the most important lesson to be taught from day one. So that we will be able to create an amazing and wonderful world for us filled with unconditional love and unlimited compassion, free from all kinds of fears, worries, and anxieties. No limitations. No restrictions. No expectations but complete freedom to do anything we want in life.

Life Is To Enjoy

If life is to be enjoyed, why do people suffer? Most of us think that life is filled with suffering. We believe this, and so we suffer in life instead of enjoying it as God intended. Moreover, the media also keeps talking about how life is very hopeless. They say so, not because they are very concerned about us, but because they want to do business using all the hopelessness they create. Those who believe in such hopelessness in various aspects of life will suffer as a result. But, those who trust in God will be blessed irrespective of their circumstances, and they will just be enjoying every moment in every aspect of life.

For example, a fear is created with respect to various diseases, and people who believe in this will be filled with fear about those diseases. Then their body will reveal what they feared, and they will suffer from those diseases. Sometimes they ask people to avoid certain foods, saying they are bad for their health, when they are actually good for us. Then, after avoiding the foods, people get affected by deficiencies created in the body as a result of avoiding those foods. Then they become sick and go for treatment. This is their business.

What happens when a person trusts God and listens to Him speak in their conscience? They will be enabled to know about all these things by various means provided by God. As they become aware of this, they will continue to eat all kinds of necessary foods without avoiding them. God will enable them to eat healthily by speaking with them in their conscience. He will encourage them to have faith in Him and not fear anything, even if the whole world is living in fear. They will be in excellent health and will have nothing to fear or worry about in life.

The media keeps talking about how hopeless the economy is and how people should always live in fear about their economy. All the insurance and investment businesses work in this manner. People are filled with fear about their future and start investing so much that they have nothing left to enjoy life with what they have. But people who trust in God will listen to His loving voice in their conscience and live in abundance, even if they do not have insurance or investments. They will be able to enjoy life irrespective of their circumstances. Their lives are filled with hope and excitement.

In the same way, some spread hopelessness about various aspects of life. They keep people from thinking and following their passions. They make people choose the same kind of life and make them feel that they are not good enough if they do not follow the general pattern. People get confused and try very hard to be like everyone else in spite of being created to be unique by their creator. They become depressed and dejected in life, and they live in unhappiness. But the people who trust in God will be able to enjoy their lives free from all these kinds of limitations, restrictions, and expectations. They will be who they are irrespective of their circumstances, where everyone follows the same pattern of life. They are not afraid to be different.

Is there hope for the people who become sick and those who live in fear about their future? Yes, of course. God loves us too much to leave us with our fears, worries, and anxieties. He is not angry about their choices, as He has created us with freedom of choice. He knows they make bad decisions because they are unaware of His love for them. So, He is just waiting for them to realise their wrong choices and turn back to Him. He will restore them to their original nature, as intended by God. He will enable them to enjoy life by listening to His loving voice in their conscience and making right choices every moment of their lives. He will enable them to live free from all kinds of sickness and fear. They shall enjoy a life of abundance in every aspect of their lives through the amazing love of God.

God Is There For You

After reading this book, you would have realised that God is not in a specific place. He is everywhere. There is no place where He is not present. We may have imagined Him to be in a place because various religions declare Him to be in various places such as heaven, worship places, mountains, rivers, trees, and so on. He is so loving and kind that He has given us all the authority over our lives to create whatever we want in them. We can create heaven or hell right where we are. Our thoughts are very powerful and have the potential to create anything. Next come our words, and finally our deeds. All these things create everything in our lives.

Even if we have created hell in our lives because of our ignorance of all these things, He loves us too much to leave us there. He desires for us to realise our wrong choices, which were also definitely made in ignorance, and turn back to Him. Trust Him with our lives at every moment and create heaven by making the right choices. Hence, it is very important to understand that God is not a dictator. But He is the most loving person, filled with unconditional love and unlimited compassion for everything He created. We need to realise that He is Love and does everything in love. If we realise this, we will also be filled with unconditional love and unlimited compassion for everyone and everything around us. We will also do everything in love. We have been created to be like Him. Let us be like Him in His nature, as described below, and enable Him to experience amazing life through us.

God loves to bless you every moment.

God loves to protect you every moment.

God loves to experience your life with you every moment.

God loves to heal and restore you every moment.

God loves to do everything with you every moment.

God loves to honour you every moment.

God loves to keep you happy and excited every moment.

God loves to talk with you every moment.

God loves to empower you every moment.

God loves to guide you every moment.

God loves to just be with you every moment.

God loves to prosper you every moment.

God loves to watch you every moment.

God loves to support you every moment.

God loves to comfort you every moment.

You can add to this to whatever you have realised Him to do for you. God should be experienced in life, and not just believed in and trusted.

He is there for you forever.

Note to beloved readers:- If you have any questions about the things you read in this book, feel free to mail me at sarah.10966marg@gmail.com

9 798888 596417